Pop Biographies

SADIE SINK
STRANGER THINGS SCENE STEALER

by Elizabeth Andrews

WELCOME TO DiscoverRoo!

This book is filled with videos, puzzles, games, and more! Scan the QR codes* while you read, or visit the website below to make this book pop.

popbooksonline.com/sink

abdobooks.com

Published by Pop!, a division of ABDO, PO Box 398166, Minneapolis, Minnesota 55439. Copyright © 2024 by Abdo Consulting Group, Inc. International copyrights reserved in all countries. No part of this book may be reproduced in any form without written permission from the publisher. DiscoverRoo™ is a trademark and logo of Pop!.

Printed in the United States of America, North Mankato, Minnesota.

052023
082023

THIS BOOK CONTAINS RECYCLED MATERIALS

Cover Photo: Getty Images
Interior Photos: Shutterstock Images, Getty Images, J G Netter/Lionsgate/Kobal/Shutterstock, Netflix/Kobal/Shutterstock, Alamy Stock Photos
Editor: Grace Hansen
Series Designer: Colleen McLaren

Library of Congress Control Number: 2022950567

Publisher's Cataloging-in-Publication Data
Names: Andrews, Elizabeth, author.
Title: Sadie Sink: Stranger Things scene stealer / by Elizabeth Andrews
Other title: Stranger Things scene stealer
Description: Minneapolis, Minnesota : Pop!, 2024 | Series: Pop biographies | Includes online resources and index
Identifiers: ISBN 9781098244392 (lib. bdg.) | ISBN 9781098245092 (ebook)
Subjects: LCSH: Sink, Sadie--Juvenile literature. | Television actors and actresses--United States--Biography--Juvenile literature. | Stranger things (Television program)--Juvenile literature. | Actors--Juvenile literature.
Classification: DDC 782.42166092--dc23

*Scanning QR codes requires a web-enabled smart device with a QR code reader app and a camera.

TABLE OF CONTENTS

CHAPTER 1
Shooting for the Stars. 4

CHAPTER 2
Sadie On Screen. 10

CHAPTER 3
Stranger than Sadie 18

CHAPTER 4
Just the Beginning. 24

Making Connections. 30
Glossary 31
Index. 32
Online Resources 32

CHAPTER 1
SHOOTING FOR THE STARS

Sadie Elizabeth Sink was born on April 14, 2002, in Brenham, Texas. She has three older brothers and a younger sister. Sadie's mother was a teacher, and her father was a football coach. Sadie's family loved sports. But Sadie was interested in a different path.

WATCH A VIDEO HERE!

Like many children, Sadie liked watching YouTube. Little did her family know, it would lead her down a life-changing path!

Annie first hit Broadway in 1977!

Sadie became interested in acting after watching Broadway videos on YouTube. She started taking acting classes at nine years old. Around the same time, Sadie began performing at Houston's Theatre Under the Stars. She starred in *White Christmas* and played Annie in *Annie*.

The Sink family could tell how talented Sadie was. They moved to New Jersey to support her. It was closer to New York City which had more theater acting opportunities. Quickly, Sadie earned her spot on Broadway's professional stages. She again starred in *Annie* playing the parts of both Annie and Duffy.

Sadie was 12 when she starred in Annie *on Broadway! She sang and danced in the show.*

Helen Mirren won a 2013 Tony Award for her role as Queen Elizabeth II in The Audience.

Sadie starred as young Queen Elizabeth II in Broadway's *The Audience*. It was one of her strongest roles yet. She worked alongside well-respected actor, Helen Mirren. Sadie was able to learn a lot from Mirren. Her acting skills got better.

Broadway theaters have audiences of at least 500 people a night!

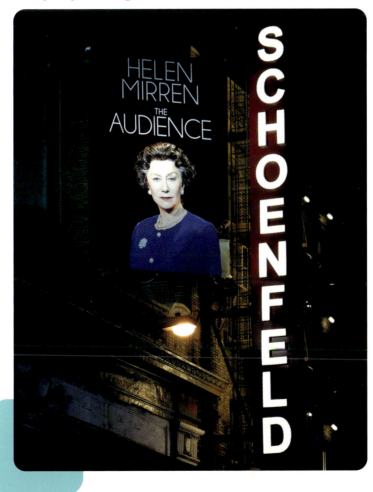

CHAPTER 2

SADIE ON SCREEN

While Sadie was making a name for herself on stage, she tried her hand in television and movies too. Between 2013 and 2016, she had one-episode roles in *The Americans*, *Blue Bloods*, and *Unbreakable Kimmy Schmidt*.

LEARN MORE HERE!

In 2015, she landed a long-term role in the international military **drama**, American Odyssey.

Sadie played a younger version of the main character in The Glass Castle. *Her character's name was Lori.*

The first films Sadie was cast in were *Chuck* and *The Glass Castle*. Both were emotional dramas based on real-life stories. In each movie, Sadie shared the

The Glass Castle had a large cast. Each of the three main characters had two younger versions of themselves.

screen with award-winning actors. They included Brie Larson and Elisabeth Moss. Sadie continued to grow her acting skills during each filming.

Sadie started getting a lot of attention for her red carpet looks when she joined Stranger Things.

In 2016, Sadie took on a role that would define her career for the next several years. At 14 years old, Sadie Sink was cast as Max Mayfield in the hit Netflix **fantasy-horror**-drama *Stranger Things*.

Sadie was excited for this role, but also a little nervous. She joined *Stranger Things* in its second season. The main cast members were her age. They had already formed friendships and connections. Sadie was able to find her place among them. She became close friends with the entire cast.

The kids in Stranger Things *live in Hawkins, Indiana, in the 1980s. They battle against creatures and forces from the Upside Down.*

Max Mayfield is a skateboarding tomboy from California. When she moves to Hawkins, Indiana, she catches the attention of the close-knit friend group called the "Party." They were impressed by Max's arcade skills. She quickly becomes friends with Eleven, Dustin, Will, Lucas, and Mike.

The Party likes to play the role-playing game Dungeons & Dragons.

CHAPTER 3

STRANGER THAN SADIE

Sadie's *Stranger Things* storyline started out slow compared to other characters on the show. When season three of *Stranger Things* came around, Max's character got a chance to **develop**. Her stepbrother Billy Hargrove becomes **possessed** by a monster called the Mind Flayer.

EXPLORE LINKS HERE!

Stranger Things has won many awards, including Best Show in 2018! Dacre Montgomery (right) plays Max's stepbrother Billy.

DID YOU KNOW?

Stranger Things has been **nominated** three times for the Screen Actors Guild Awards' Outstanding Performance by an Ensemble in a **Drama** Series. The show has won it once!

In *Stranger Things* season four, Sadie's character goes through a lot. After the death of her stepbrother, Max's family falls apart. She also experiences **post-traumatic stress disorder** (PTSD) and becomes the target of the terrible monster Vecna. Sadie proved how great of an actor she was in the fourth season. **Critics** and her fans applauded her emotional performance.

Max Mayfield is always listening to music in season four.

The song "Running Up That Hill" by Kate Bush helped Max Mayfield deal with her PTSD. The use of it in season four brought new attention to the 1985 song.

The COVID-19 pandemic shut down filming for season four of *Stranger Things*. The cast and crew had to take a year-and-a-half break. Sadie thought the extra time with the script helped her deepen her connection to Max and what her character was going through. She believed the break helped her overall performance.

THREE MOVIES.
THREE WEEKS.
ONE KILLER STORY.

CAMP NIGHTWINGS

A FILM TRILOGY EVENT

FEAR STREET

Sadie was a star for Netflix. The company cast her to play Ziggy Berman in the second and third films of the *Fear Street* trilogy. Again, Sadie received critical **acclaim** for her performance in the **horror** movies.

SADIE + MAX

Filming season four of *Stranger Things* was very emotional. Sadie listened to a lot of music by the artist Kate Bush to prepare for her role. She got strength from Max's bravery and courage. Sadie gave a great performance. All of her hard work helped her during the terrifying scene where Max is running from Vecna. Some say it's the best scene in the entire series.

The **Fear Street** *movies are based on books written by famous author R.L. Stine.*

CHAPTER 4

JUST THE BEGINNING

In 2021, Sadie again moved beyond Netflix shows and movies. To her fans' delight, she was selected to play the lead in Taylor Swift's *All Too Well: The Short Film*. The film, which was released on YouTube, was watched more than 32 million times

COMPLETE AN ACTIVITY HERE!

DID YOU KNOW? Taylor Swift only imagined Sadie playing the main female role in her short film. If Sadie hadn't agreed to play the part, Taylor said she likely would not have made the film.

in three days. **Critics** were impressed with the emotion Sadie brought to the screen.

Sadie's costars in the short film included Dylan O'Brien and Taylor Swift.

Sadie Sink took on another emotional role in the 2022 film called *The Whale*. Her character Ellie is an angry, loud, and aggressive teenager dealing with a difficult relationship with her dad. Ellie is very different compared to Sadie who is kindhearted, soft-spoken, and close to her family.

Sadie Sink and her costars Brendan Fraser and Hong Chau were **nominated** for many awards.

Brendan Fraser won the Academy Award for Best Actor for his performance in The Whale.

Sadie is an animal rights activist. This means she takes action to make sure all animals are treated well.

Along with acting, Sadie is passionate about animal rights and welfare. She uses her social media pages to teach her fans about **veganism**. She also works hard to support animal rescue organizations based in New York.

The world loves Sadie Sink and everything she does. At just 20 years old, Sadie has a long list of movie, TV, and theater credits. Sadie said she enjoys the challenges of acting and getting to be someone else for a period of time. Her list of roles will keep growing. The sky is the limit for this superstar!

Stranger Things *would end after its fifth season. Sadie said it will be hard to leave the show behind.*

MAKING CONNECTIONS

TEXT-TO-SELF

Sadie Sink started performing for crowds of more than 500 people when she was 12. How would you feel performing in front of that many people?

TEXT-TO-TEXT

Have you read any other books about actors? If so, how were those actors similar to or different from Sadie Sink?

TEXT-TO-WORLD

Sadie Sink wants animals all over the world to be treated better. She's an animal activist. What would you like to see change for the better in the world? Please explain your answer.

GLOSSARY

acclaim — praise.

critic — a person who writes opinions about music, movies, plays, books, and television shows.

develop — to gain more personality, depth, and motivation as a character.

drama — a serious play, movie, or television show.

fantasy — a play, movie, or television show that involves magic or imaginative elements.

horror — a play, movie, or television show that frightens or scares the audience.

nominated — chosen as a possible winner for an award.

possessed — controlled or affected by an outside evil force.

post-traumatic stress disorder — often shortened to PTSD, a mental sickness that causes a person to feel a lot of emotional and physical distress when exposed to situations that remind them of a troubling event.

veganism — not eating any animal products including meat, dairy products, and eggs.

INDEX

animal rights, 28
All Too Well: The Short Film, 24–25
Annie, 6–7
Audience, The, 8–9

Broadway, 6–9

Chuck, 12–13
critics, 20, 23, 25

family, 4, 7
Fear Street (films), 23

Glass Castle, The, 12–13

New Jersey, 7

Stranger Things, 14–15, 17–18, 20–21, 23

Texas, 4, 6

Whale, The, 27

DiscoverRoo!
ONLINE RESOURCES

This book is filled with videos, puzzles, games, and more! Scan the QR codes* while you read, or visit the website below to make this book pop.

popbooksonline.com/sink

*Scanning QR codes requires a web-enabled smart device with a QR code reader app and a camera.